ELEPHANTS OF THE WORLD: FUN FACTS ABOUT ELEPHANTS

SPEEDY
PUBLISHING

Speedy Publishing LLC
40 E. Main St. #1156
Newark, DE 19711
www.speedypublishing.com

There are two recognized species of elephants, the African elephant and the Asian elephant.

Elephants are the largest land-living mammal in the world. They have long noses, large ears and thick legs. Their tusks can be up to 10 feet long.

A young elephant is called a calf. Like all mammals the babies feed off their mother's milk.

Elephants use their long trunks to pick up food as small as a blade of grass. They also use their trunk to drink, smell, and suck up water to spray themselves for a bath.

Elephants are extremely intelligent animals. Elephants can remember routes to watering holes over incredibly long stretches of time.

Elephants are herbivorous
and can be found in different
habitats including savannahs,
forests, deserts and marshes.

Elephants have poor eyesight, but excellent hearing and sense of smell. They can hear each other's calls up to 5 miles away.

Made in the USA
San Bernardino, CA
23 April 2019